The Love That I Love
By
De'Borah Raquel

Artistic Introduction: Poetry saying Hello

I'm figuring that since you love music
You'll love poetry too
As an artist
In love with art
Perhaps you can appreciate the art of these words:
Poetry is simply the rhythm of music
Slightly lacking the melody
The beat still rocks
Be still... rock
I've concluded from hearing your heavenly voice
Seeing your natural beauty
Ability, agility, masculinity
That perhaps God
Should have punished the angels
A bit more severely
For having touched the daughters of man
For the traces of angel in you
Lead me to believe
They have not yet learned their lesson
I do not find fault with them
Rather find myself blessed by their transgressions
I understand
From where you were created
Beauty, music, love
Would be the process of creation
So as opposed to saying
I love you
I'll say that I love your music
Your performance
I like the you
You are in public
But am more curious
About the you
You are
When no one else is around
I suppose I'd be saying

Although I love the instruments
Which enhance the song of your soul
I'm more concerned with the lyrics
What your song sounds like bare
Your soul a cappella
I think that's what I mean
If you were music
I'd be poetry
I'd be in you
We'd go together
To/get/**Her**
Because if you love music
The way I think you do
The way I love poetry
Then **Her**
Would be *Life*
And isn't that what we are seeking?
Poetry
Saying hello

The Search to Find Me

When I've searched for myself in everything
On the empty stage
In seas of words
In a classroom, teaching or learning
There is one place I can look to find myself
When I can't find me in anything else
In your arms is where I'd be resting
Safe from the let downs of everyday mundane occurrences
From the disappointments of heartbreak
The fear of not being GOOD enough
The fear of not being loved or wanted
Those all disappear from memory and existence
When you hold me
I could cry, love, live, die, be, fly, soar
Relax and let the world glide away in the tears of yesterday
You allow me the freedom of expression
Not silenced by presence
Your embrace is strong
A fortress to protect me from anything
The pain of my past
My thoughts of self-doubt
My critics' harsh words
Hit your surface and fall away
into the nothingness that they are
And I seek your comfort
When all else has failed me
The reflection of God's mirrored love facing each other
Infinity... and I am caught in between
Cradled and rocked slow to the lullaby of your heartbeat
In your arms is the only place that I am allowed to just be...
A poet, lover, child, woman, actress,
A singer, friend, companion, leader, student,
A force to be reckoned with,
Simply, your love...
I'm allowed to just be me
In your arms

So, if I'm lost
I know exactly where home would be
Buried in you
Waiting for me to find me

The Forever Prayer

"Is this forever?"
With my hand in yours
Saying words of great depth
I have waited for this moment
To promise my devotion and love
Before God, I will stand with you
Belong to you and Him alone
This moment is not forever
It is only the start of so much more
As minutes grow to hours
Hours pass to days
Days move to weeks
Weeks shift to months
Months span to years
I will love you as completely as humanly possible
"For God so loved the world that He gave..."
I will give to you until your joy can meet my own...
So is this forever?
Forever starts now
With you and me
Here together
We will serve, honor, obey, and love God
So that He may teach us
To achieve a higher love... Agape
You will lead and I will help
For where you go I shall follow
I love you...
Yesterday, Today, Tomorrow
Until forever
This is it
If it be God's will
In Jesus' name I ask and pray
Amen

Reassured Love

There is no need to rush or be afraid
My love will not flee
Like the darkness at the breaking of the dawn
It will remain constant and true
If distance causes the heart to grow fonder
Then my heart will experience a renewed joy
An ecstatic release at our reunion
I will miss you everyday
Patiently waiting for your return
Though I'd been awaiting your arrival
Long before I became aware of your existence
More than I ever hoped for
Far exceeding my expectations
Your perfect imperfections make you perfectly suited for
me
I adore you...
Everything about you makes my spirit smile
From your slight stutter when you're excited
Your sexy sweet southern speech
To your candy coated kisses
That leave me lightheaded and dizzy
Everything I've ever needed
Abundantly more than I wanted
Or could even think to ask for
This love is worth every day of waiting
Sweet slow motion moments
I relive the memories of holding you
To keep loneliness away at arms length
But I still yearn for your kiss
Scent, touch, taste...
The way you look at me
When we lay silent
No...
My love for you will not fade
With miles and time
It will only increase in quality
And grow in strength
I love you and am more than content to wait

9

When No One is Looking

I want to outstretch
These limbs called arms
Gather you into the warm
Soft comfort
Lay your head against me
Breathe you in
Until my senses go numb
I want to experience
Your entire emersion
Early...
Like fresh dew
Gracing the grass
At dawn's first peak
Feel the warmth from your body
Melt the cool air
Between soft breaths
Eyes closed
All the way deep
Squeeze tighter
Never let you go
I NEED this
Just this... moment
I need YOU
To stroke your hair lightly
As you drift
Into a world
Where my heartbeat
Is the tick/tock of time
And my breath syncs with yours
We breathe easy
Deep
I watch you
So effortlessly my Love
His love
Manifested in human form
I am touching love
When I'm touching you
His love
For me

10

In your touch
So I crave the silent hours
Spent in seclusion
When the sound
Of your heart beating
Is the only melody I hear
When I am holding you...
I just want to hold you
Today
Tomorrow
Tonight
Forever
The rest of my life
Just hold you
Just hold you...
When no one is looking

I Want a Man

I want a man
To love me like rain
Washing over me
Making me want to lie
Comforted between his thighs
Draped in blankets
I sleep peacefully
So wet when he comes
Crashing down
I put away my umbrella
And dance with the storm
Rainy day becomes lazy
And I hate him for that
But he comes often
The way that I
Want a man to
Warm me after
The rain has chilled
My bones and soaked my skin
Love me until
I can't stand you
And try to find shelter

11

That's the only love for me
Drive me insane
Make me ill
I'll flee for a while
But I'll come back
'Cause I want a man
To love me like rain
Love me like that

The Grace of Sleep

Morning breaks and I awake
The first thing I see is your beautiful face
As I watch you sleeping
So peaceful and quiet
I know that I am in love with you
Your breaths slow and steady
I'd move to hold you
But from fear of waking you
I simply watch in awe
Remember the feeling of being in your arms
The warmth of your embrace
I crave that closeness
When my bed finds me without you
So in moments of waking
With you so close to me
I know that I could spend the rest of my nights
Resting in your arms
And the remainder of my mornings by your side
Just the very act of sharing your space
I breathe your air
Experience your joy
Bask in your grace
There is no one that I want to wake up with more
So I smile in these quiet hours
While I watch you sleeping
You are unaware

The Myth of the fall

We will not fall
To fall suggests an accident
This will be intentional
Falling without the safety net
Of reciprocated love
Undoubtedly leads to injuries
Who's to say
That the safety net can sustain
The impact of the fall
There are many things to consider
If hurt in the process of falling
There is pain, a healing time
A process of recuperation
And there is no guarantee
Of a complete recovery
No... I will not fall
I will be completely aware
It will be a conscious decision
So that should I wish to stop
I will have the choice to do so
I will not fall in love
I will learn to be in love
Love being a behavior
To be learned and executed
I will not permit you to fall
You will be taught to love
And learn to be in love with me
To build with reciprocity
To understand sacrifice
To truly know love...
We cannot fall
We must stand side by side
 And enter into the altered state of being together
I will not fall, jump, run
Bend, bow, go, be pushed
I will not be left without a choice
With no defense against a fall
A mistake of love
Nor will I allow you to be a victim

Of a fall
Love will not take us down
As falls so often do
Our love will elevate our emotions, behaviors, decisions
The way that a good education will
We will not fall in
But we will learn to love

FALLING

The Process of Obsession

There are times when I catch a glimpse of love
It's in the eyes, a look that says what the lips won't
In your arms, there is a calm that I cannot describe
Yet the touch of your hand sends me into overload
I am living in the moments when you smile softly
The way that you hold your mouth when you read
The way that your voice cracks when you yell
I am waiting for the perfect moment to express my feelings
The right time to ask you to kiss me
I am living for the day when you will lean over
Take me into your arms and sweetly press your lips to mine
When you kiss me
I will taste what love might have tasted like
I might just be able to love you, still I don't expect to
I don't expect to fall for a person that is unable to
reciprocate
When I am waiting for you to kiss me, anticipation builds
to climax
And I just might get the chance to see love
I might feel it with my own lips and hands
I could touch love this time...
Maybe

The Want to Love You

What if I wanted to love you
Not at the limited capacity
Restricted by common rules of
Male and Female behavior
Which says that I have to wait
You have to make the first move
That I am powerless to aid
In my own happiness
But to love you completely...
If I wanted to love the things
You dislike about yourself
Be the light in your dark places

15

Take the ice cold
Replace it with fire
Pursue you
Enjoy you
Indulge you
Love the pain away
Love the hurt
Until it doesn't anymore...
If you could look into my eyes
See the reflection of your love
Understand that you were not intended
To live your life alone
That you could find completeness
With me...
To see that I can be your friend
Erase your suffering
Be the calm that soothes you
Your comfort when peace escapes you
That we can be silent
When you don't want to speak
We can kiss when we are alone
That we can just be
Free to love without fear or restraint
I'd be the sea to your island
The sky for you to cast your stars
To love without boundaries
I offer myself to you
To do with me as you will....
If you would let me love you
There would be nothing
That you would ask for
If it's in my power to give you
That you would go without
I'd breathe for you
Live for you
If you would let me love you
And love me back as best you could
I'll love you
I'd love you
I love you
I do

A Question of Love

Who teaches us to love?
It's God, I'm sure
What would happen
If I allowed myself to fall
If you took the time to know me
Could you love me
Would you be inspired
To take me apart
Figure out the things that make me
So odd and better than normal
Find something about me to love
Discover what provokes me to
Live, Love, Dare, Dream
Could you reciprocate
But friendship is not fair
Not to me
I think I could be falling into this
Into what "us" would be like
And if I ever could love you
The way that I hope to
Would the struggle be worth the change
I will break and love you
When does God teach you to love me?

Peach Rose

I want to experience
The simultaneous touching of lips
Something so intimate
Provocative and engaging
The penetration of it
Exchange of warmth
Slight movement of tongue
Dare to call it sexual
His mouth is inviting
I'd like to journey inside
Press mahogany to peach rose
Enjoy the friction of touch
Taste him

17

Delight in our lips
Sliding against each other
Take the delectable bottom peach rose
Between mahogany
Gently tug and release
I dream of the moment
When I will be granted
The pleasure of his kiss

Pieces of You

I steal little
Pieces of you
Keep them, lock them
Deep within my heart
Pieces of
Your life
Your essence
Need almost
Obsessively
Us in an
Embrace
Your body
Against mine
Enfold me in your arms
I steal your scent
Sweet
That beckons to
My senses
Makes me yearn
Ache
For you
Lost in every word
I steal little
Pieces of your heart
To complete my own

Real Talk: I'd say it if I had the courage

I want to know you
Become familiar with all parts
Of you and your entire person
I want to see what's beneath
Those beautiful eyes of yours
Let me see Your heart
If you dare to be so open
Help me to see You
Not the 'Mr. Friendly' that you share
With the world
Who are you in your secrets
I'm so into your mental
Impressed by your physical
Yet you remain clueless
To the thoughts your provoke
Write me into your plans
I could become
Your music and melody
You could be the lyrics
That would fill the pages
Of my books
If only you would give the word
I would leave it all
Look back for nothing
I would lose me
For the chance to know you
Just to know you...
And feel you on some deeper level

Knowing me...Knowing you

I'm looking into you
Not looking at you or past you
Just straight into you
Attempting to see you
Trying to find myself in you
Seeking an affirmation
To see if you're real
I'm trying to understand you

Not the things you do or say
Just to understand YOU
Striving to answer my questions:
Why don't we have intimate talks
About you and your life and your love?
Why are you so guarded and reserved?
I'm trying to know you
Not to like you or love you
Just want to know you
To know what makes you love
What are your passions?
What makes your eyes smile?
I'm looking into you
Seeing my reflection
Looking back into me

Give and Gain

Time has not yet healed my wounds of yesteryear
I have not resolved to know him again
Though he may swear his undying love
Neither can I see nor feel this love
I hear simple words
They bear no weight
For his actions have long proved contrary to his sweet
sounding words
And even though the words sound good
Their bitter taste of reality causes my stomach to boil
He is a liar!
A selfish, hypocritical, cowardly liar!
I owe him nothing of myself
Yet he requests my friendship as if it were due him
I feel as though I wasted myself on him
Spent my money, time, and love
All to yield no return
Leaving me to question
What all did I really give him
Or what from him did I really gain

Nonexistent

I have been foolish to dwell on you
For these past many months
I as a woman do not exist for you
And have been advised to forget about you
I've allowed myself to conceive feelings
For a man that will not reciprocate
You have fooled most people
Had me convinced to ignore my instincts
But I know the truth now
Didn't trust me enough to be honest
Did you think I would look at you differently
The most beautiful man
I've ever known

Tell me you know I'm not shallow
Nor am I closed-minded
You...
We would have been better friends
And I could have saved myself
The agony of wanting you
The embarrassment of pursuing you
Why didn't you stop me
Did you enjoy your charade
I will say that I am thankful
Thankful for the inspiration
For the pain of wanting the unattainable
Truth hurt so bad that it made my journal cry
I wanted to love you
To give you everything
And I cry because I know
You cannot exist for me...
As a lover

That Bitch

That bitch had me up all night
Made me cry myself to sleep
I wanted to be her friend
But that bitch kept trying to fight me
She convinced me to drown my sorrows
Until every swallow burned my chest
I sat outside of his house for hours
Because she said that he'd be there
That bitch had me going
I was all caught out there
Looking foolishly stupid
After writing poem after poem
Sending gift after gift
That bitch betrayed me
Decided that I should be left wanting
Made nice with everyone but me
In pursuit of the dreams I once hoped for
I sought her out
She denied my advances
Ignored my pleas

Laughed at my questions
In the struggle to understand her
I found myself unrecognizable
Insecure, jealous, hateful
That bitch changed me
I spent thousands of dollars in her name
Spoon-fed sweet summer soft lies
Swallowed and became full
But the aftertaste left me on my knees
Clutching a plastic bag
Regurgitating the promises she made me
At times she made me happy
Smile until my cheeks hurt
Other times she'd beat me until my eyes swelled shut
Finally, I gave up on that bitch
I hogtied, gagged, and stuffed her ass in the closet
But her sweet soft cries would not let me sleep
So I freed her mouth and allowed her to speak...
She said "Please, let me out! I'll be right this time
You can trust me, I won't hurt you..."
That bitch, that bitch, that bitch...
Called Love

For a Friend

I hurt for him
So bad that the tears
He refused to shed
Trickled down my cheeks
I've been there
Too sad to cry
Sleep deprived but not for the lack of trying
Lose the will to eat
But when you do
Nourishments turn to rot
Leaving you clutching the toilet seat
Longing to die
Yet too afraid of death
I know it hurts
So we gain new addictions
Attempting to get over our lost loves

Burying ourselves deeper in denial
Because we aren't done until we're done
Haven't had enough until it's too much
I feel his pain
Feel my heart breaking the same way
Over and over again
Knowing that I can do nothing
Except wait for his deliverance
Wait for him to be broken
So that God can fix him
Heartbreak is a sad and lonely thing
It can make you crazy if you let it
And he thinks that I don't know how it feels...
If only he knew
I know those feelings all too well

Break-Up

Checked my pride at the door
Left my vanity in the car
Sarcasm in my bag
(Just in case I need it)
Put my sanity under my pillow
So I can find it the next time I want it
Got insecurity splotched on my t-shirt
Anger-flavored lip gloss
With low-rise self esteem jeans
Falling over cold feet running shoes
Hid my faith in the bible in my bottom drawer
under the porn
Gave my courage to my sister
'cause she needed it one night
But she never gave it back
Stuffed my intuition in the back of the closet
Forgot my rationale outside
with an empty case of Jack Daniels
On your sidewalk
Placed my heart in your hands...
Wait a minute...
The tears in my eyes are the only things that are

Where they should be
This is how I came equipped for the break-up

Better

As I lay in his bed
I can think of nothing but she
Making false love
An imitation of me
She will never compare
I am infinitely her superior
And his too
Girls who like leftovers
Man that likes it loose
We weren't ready for this love
And I wasn't ready for the burn
But she can't love like me
Her eyes don't glow like this
I made him last forever
So she could steal my Greek king
But people are not possessions
Chasing the love that chose another
I am better than that
And her too

Box of Memories

I've got multiple boxes of you
One box of boys, friends
Boyfriends of the past
Have found their way into that box
Not you
Your fate is not in that box
Something else waits for you
I could pack away the pictures
The gifts that you gave me
Old movie stubs
Journals and poems
Containing your name
But it would not matter
Couldn't just put you away

Like I had done the others
You would linger
From songs on the radio
To the different holidays
You would remain
I've got you in my blood
The silent poison
That kills for years
No
You won't be in that box
You'll be trapped in my mind
As long as I have memory

UNREQUITED

Disclaimer

I never said things should be perfect
I never thought they would be
I just thought things should be simple
Make sense
Easy to comprehend
The situation of Boy meets Girl
They like
They lust
They love
Should be that simple
But it isn't
Girl sees Boy
Boy sees Girl
Girl and Boy lust for each other
Girl pursues Boy
Girl loves Boy
Boy ignores Girl
Relationship is twisted gains
Games played by players
With little to no rules
Love and Life forgot to include the instructions
That was not what I consented to
I wanted something worth having
Worth working for
Worth a sacrifice
I wanted him
And all that he personified
But he did not counter
This is nowhere near what makes sense
At least not to me

Private Prayer

Every time I say his name
It is a prayer unto God
I say it aloud
Simply for the sake of hearing it
A sweet song
Sung into my heart
Palms pressed together
I pray
If he's real, let me touch him
Hold him until his hurts
Are no longer in existence
If he's only a glimpse of my dreams
I pray for incessant rest
So that I can be near him
Extended periods of time
I think he might be
What heaven looks and feels like
But if he isn't
I know he must be a close second
And maybe heaven is worth being good for after all
Everything about him is poetry
Smooth and delicate
Intimate and intricate
That I could delight in all day
God, why let me...
Torture myself?

Give a Voice to it

I love you...
My silent thoughts
Read across the page so loud
That I can hear them
As if I had spoken the words
But my lips are motionless
I want you to love me back
Love the parts of me that ache,
Bleed, cry, think, love

Until I don't hurt anymore
The words develop an alto voice tone
And sing the truth onto
Your deaf ears
I plead, with my persuasive techniques
For the truth to stop
Spilling from my lips
Through my hands
Onto the paper scarred by lead
You can't hear me
Because I haven't said it aloud
I do love you
Still

Chasing Thoughts about Tomorrow

I'm absolutely insane
I hurt inside
Anything and everything
I'd be a liar
If I said that I was not afraid
We're young
You're unsure
I'm scared
Stubborn and headstrong
I won't back down
I won't give you up
I'll let you go
But I'll never stop
You're what I've waited for
And now...
Now, I'm not even sure
I used to be
But now, I don't know
It's alright
Because you don't
Seem to know anything
About us either
I wish that I could follow you
That you could get me
That we could

Get us together
Find the place
Where love
Is all that matters
It's much too late
To try and not
Make me love you
As I'm trying to escape
This will hurt
Close your eyes
And try not to look
If it's over
Then it's over
Let's not cry
Let's just enjoy
The love that once was
You and I
Am not complete
Without you
But we can't stay
Not like this
Let's chase the moon
Sing to the stars
Write about tomorrow
Yesterday
And let's just have
Right now
I do love you
Forever
Would you dream
My dreams
Love me
Until you can
Touch sound
When you can
Taste a picture
And when you can
Be sure
That this is all
That you've never wanted
But so much more than you need

Maybe we can do this
Another time
Perhaps

Wishful Reciprocation

When there is nothing left to be said
After I've kissed you for the thousandth time
While I watch you sleeping
As you lie in my arms with tears in your eyes...
When we hold hands
After we've shared an intimate moment
While enthralled in an embrace
As our eyes meet from across the table...
When you kiss me uncontrollably
After you and I have argued
While you laugh at me
As we talk about God and love...
When you read to me aloud
After I've cried for hours
While you tickle me all over
As you smile and shake your head ...
When I first wake up
After I hear your voice
While we watch the sunset
As we watch the moonlight on the ocean...
When you call my name
After I've written you another poem
While you remain unaware
As you accept my gifts...
When I am trembling
After you have walked away
While I am longing to have you hold me
As I attempt to fade into you...
I will confess the entire truth
 I am fearful of the love I feel for you
 I know your feelings are not the equal of my own
That I am desperately wanting...
Helplessly, hopelessly, undeniably
In love with you

Confession of an Addict: on a Social Network

I thought of removing him from my list of friends
It becomes painful to see him every day
The temptation to send him messages
To check on his status
I resist the lure of curiosity
His picture taunts me
Serving as a constant reminder of things that I can't have
As if I could ever forget...
Slowly I push him to the far corners of memory
Let him fade into the past
While the cravings lessen
I let the hope of he and I
Whither away into the nothingness of our friendship
Desire dying under the pressure of truth...
He wants nothing of me
The process is slow and steady
With many pitfalls and sinkholes
Living in denial like an addict
He being my hallucinogen of choice
His scent producing the sensations of an inhalant
I must have imagined the past two years
Every memory and thought of he and I
Maintain distortion
I cannot trust my mind to produce accurate memories
So I attempt to forget the fabricated past
With rapid detoxification
Tightly pressed and strapped into the straightjacket of
reality
I had to have gone crazy
Becoming a junkie of imagined drugs
Heavily sedated on wishes
No longer intoxicated
I am sober
Recovering slowly with grace and poise
I am clean 21 days and counting

Love suffers... for how long?

I love him like
Yesterday's tears
Cried long and hard
Drenching Today's hopes
From the pain he'll cause Tomorrow

I love him like
Three days gone
Without water
In Texas July heat
Depleted and defeated, I thirst

I love him like
Autumn too soon ended
Colors faded
Into the silent trees
Dead with Winter's snow

I love him like
Everyday never ending
Sweet and sour Summer pomegranates'
Juice dripping from his lips
Escaping the words I wish he'd say...

"I'm in love with you"

Crystal Clear Vision

I wish you could see yourself
The way that I see you
You possess the power to make me laugh
When I am in mourning
And the ability to make me cry
At the most joyful occasion
I see a beautiful brown woman
Full of vision, hopes, and dreams
I see the vibrant brilliance on the inside
That you only see in your hair
The truth is always present in your eyes
As it passes over your lips
You are so much more than you see
Dig deeper and discover
What I realized years ago
You are the irreplaceable puzzle piece
The truth that must be heard
The woman that others hate in public
And worship behind your back
You are talent...
God's gifts to the visionless world
So I am thankful
Because He let me see you first
For who you really are
And not for who you see
Look into yourself
Through the eyes of another
So that you can finally see
What the world has been seeing
All along

A love Poem For Michelle
Dedicated to Michelle Elaine Carter Wongus

I love your voice
Strong sounding swooning strumming
The drums of my ears
Until I am lost
In every word that you say
I love the way you laugh
Loud, luxurious, lively
Bent over with your chest in your lap
Until tears stream your cheeks
I love to watch you
Writing, working, walking
With such a zest for all that you do
That I am in awe just to see what you'll do next
I love the way that you love Antoine
Fully, fortified, fortunate, faithful
So completely that I know God predestined it
I pray to be as blessed with my mate
I love your strength
Amazing, affirming, astounding
With your actions and words
That I am speechless
I love your family
Talented, talkative, thriving, thrilling
To the point that I feel I belong
And you wouldn't have it any other way
I love the way that you love God
Worshipping, waiting, walking, working
The way that God is all in you
And speaks to me from your words
But more than anything that I love about you...
I love YOU!
More than my pretty witty words
Or my right aligned poems
I love YOU!
For all that you are
A mother, poet, lover, actress, performer
Sister, aunt, niece, cousin, daughter, friend
Wife, protector, defender, educator, innovator

Scholar, soldier, survivor, servant, Christian, counselor...
I love that you don't hurt anymore
I love that you have peace
I love that you are in heaven
I love that you are in heaven
I love that you are in heaven...
With My God
I love YOU!
And I'm sure
I am not the only one.

Gifted

God allows me to get away with
Saying sweet sounding words
Blessed me with something special
Though I acknowledge my nothingness
He gives me everything
I lack the full knowledge of His grace
And only understand that I feel it
So effortlessly experience His comfort
He gives me such soul saving joy
In times of pain, He grants me ease
When I've cried until I can't breathe
God is the first breath that I regain
I know of His gifts
Am so fortunate that He smiles on me
Still I deserve none of His mercies
It's only the blood of Jesus
That allows me to speak
Hold favor with our Father
I am gifted
Because God gave to me
He gives to me
He lives in me
Amen, Amen, Amen

The Other's Best Friend

He needed someone to love him
Someone to appreciate his gifts
Talented and tormented
By the past he made attempts
To drink away
He needed understanding
The kind of man that women pray for
Intelligent, spiritual
Adored by women and men alike
In need of a type of love
The kind only a woman can give
He stood apart from the others
Unafraid to be vulnerable
Bold enough to cry
Wise enough to pray
He was phenomenal...
He was intensely lonely
Beautifully miserable
And I felt such compassion for him
Saw so much of myself in him
Experienced his needs
Understood his love
How he didn't think he'd ever find
A woman capable of receiving
The kind of love that he would give her
In him I found a like-minded companion
Unaware that I was his counterpart
And I loved him
Not in a sexual way
But in a way that has no gender
Without being judgmental
Without casting stones
So we sat back on the sofa
Listening to *Damien sing
Knocking back drinks
Discussing our beliefs
While the other, his best friend \ my lover
Slept only a few feet before us
Oblivious

*Damien- reference to Damien Rice (singer, songwriter, musician)

Beautiful Breeze Bliss

I lay in the warm glow of the sun
See the pale-blue sky
Sprinkled by linen-white birds
In that moment, I know there is a God
That He created the beauty of the earth
Simply for me to behold and enjoy
As He extends my comfort during my search for comfort
I experience peace during my stress
Joy in my time of grief
God blesses me so effortlessly
Bestowed upon me a talent with words
A gift of performance
With the ability to love
The only proof of God I need
Is to simply look at myself
The beauty of my eyes
Sees the beauty of the world
And that is proof enough that God is marvelous
In this beautiful breeze bliss
That God has granted me the privilege
The very honor of experiencing
I cannot sit and be ignorant
He is God
And I, His own creation

Virginia the Beautiful

I am between mountains
Grinding slowly down winding roads
Suspended in valleys
Staring at skies of powder blue
Lean my head against the window
Hair blows whipping my face
I gaze at mashed potato clouds
Inhale the fresh mountain air
Ears pop in the change of elevation

Take in the beautiful view
I am blessed
We ride through beauty
She touches my eyes
Quenches my thirst for more
As her enchanting grace closes in around me
Deep in her valleys
I sigh
She is lovely
And God is with her
For beauty like that only exists through one creator
We cruise through her mountains
Blanketed by the sky
She is home to me
The beautiful Virginia
Deep and lovely
With sandy beaches
Hidden valleys
Mountainsides of green
I am safe
Lost in her beautiful charm
Virginia and me

God's Love: In my sisters' eyes

What if I could love you
The way that God loves you?
I know that my human heart
Could never do you justice
But I am ever striving
To love you over and over again
I love the way your tears fall
Down your smooth cheeks
Though I hate to see you cry
I love to see the human side of you
Seem so perfect in every way that I am not
Though I put my heart in your hands
Only when I know that you cannot break it
I indulge in the pure joy of your love
When you love me
Although I find that I am often unable

To show you the fondest admiration
That I feel towards you
God knows that I pray
To love you the way that He does
His plans for you far exceed my own
Well wishes for your life
You may fight my love
I may hurt you unintentionally
In the struggle to become
One sisterhood united under Christ
But we will get there
We will get there
You will love me
I will love you
Until Christ sets fire to the earth
This bond shall not be parted

ENDLESS

If The Moment Never Comes

When every room is cold
When I'm screaming into my pillow
I know that I am not crazy
The times that we embrace
When you laugh at me just being me
When you stare at me from behind long lashes
When you watch me sleeping
When you realize that you love me
I will know that I have not gone mad
I'm not angry about our situation
I'm angry about my feelings
The fact that I can't change them today
If you didn't love me
I could make you out to be
The cretin that I imagine you
Allow myself to play the helpless victim
Of the love that we once shared
But you do love me
On some level
I know it's true
What I am waiting for is the moment
You will deserve to have me
When you will feel love for what it is
When you won't take advantage of me
When you will love and adore me
The way that I love you
But that day has yet to come

Flooded

Tonight I'm restless
The sky fell before my eyes
Tears that heaven cried were never ceasing
So I tried to salvage the moment
Before it passed
I grabbed your hand and you and I

41

Ran outside to mend our bodies with the pavement
Head to head on our backs
The rain danced over my face
"Don't close your eyes"
You say to me
Letting heaven's tears flush my eyes
Soaked and saturated
We chased the storm
Because we weren't totally clean
The fallen sky made the act pure
And the storm washed over us
As you flooded into me

Living in the Moment

Will you lie with me
Just for tonight
Until tomorrow
I would hold you close
In my eyes
You are frightened
I am silent
We will get through this
Everything will be alright
In your arms
Time ceases movement
Suspended in motion
Where you are broken
I will try to fix you
Alive inside of me
Flexing curves arching back
Am incoherent
Deaf and nearly blind
All I see in your eyes
Our gardens attempting to bloom
Flourish with the heat and rain
Fall limp with autumn's breeze
Your winter dies inside of me
Eyes flutter shut
We dance and I am breathless

Afraid that like will grow to love
Love fade to hurt
To love you once more
Gain comprehension
I know you'll say "no"
But I ask anyway...
Will you lie with me
Just for tonight
Until tomorrow
I would hold you close
In my eyes
In your arms
Tomorrow will never come
At least not for me

Effect: A Delayed Reaction

He was almost honest
But refused to admit fear
Preventing me from easing his doubt
I wanted to soothe him
Tell him that I wouldn't hurt him
Hold him so gently
Effortlessly inspire his will to love
Divulge vanilla flavored secret kisses
He disabled my ability to tell the truth
To be honest about my intentions
I wanted to say anything
Make him feel everything
That I experienced in his kiss
Honey-coated syllables
Chocolate-covered words
I could not give more of myself
Because he was guarded
Denying the possibilities:
He could need me
Grant me the power to affect him
I could be special
We could...
He was reserved

Like the last copy
Of my favorite poetry book
On the top shelf
In the non-fiction section/ but for who?
I wanted to reach the unavoidable end
I could love him
I am capable
I would if he were willing to teach me
But he refused to admit fear
Preventing me from experiencing him
In his entirety

The Mechanics of The Kiss

Eyes close
Lips gently press to lips
Mouths open to speak
Then find themselves silenced
At the new tastes
Tongues touch and pass
Lips slide and move to feel more
Soft sucks and delicate bites
French vanilla candy kisses
Warm cinnamon spice
Cool winter-icy-fresh flavors
Mixing and melting
Half open
Half-closed mouths
Breathing sweetly
Exchanging the life of this
Anticipated, forever lasting
Short-lived moment
Of being ever consumed
In a curious way
Of displaying a sign of life
There's more to be sought
So bodies engage
Only to satisfy the desires of the lips' dance
Thumbs move to chin
As index fingers rest on jaw line
Hands pull torso in closer

To gain complete fulfillment
As this oral intercourse
Becomes more intimate and intense
Than the process of climax
The tongues retreat
And lips subside
Clouded eyes become open and clear
The moment has passed
As is this kiss ended

Beautiful disaster

Love: my beautiful disaster
Ruined my semi-charmed existence
Disturbed my carnal party
Convicted me of innocent crimes
He came in and I was different
Slowed my destructive behavior to cessation
My intentions were good
To be friends
Nothing else...
Then I wasn't sure anymore
There I was... falling in love
With this man/boy
I reserved to give him nothing
Let him love me and give nothing of myself
Not going to do this again
I'm sick of love
Vomit my meals
Inadequate amounts of sleep
By definition means that I am not sane
I'm not
I am crazy
In love with a child
His biological age calls him a man
But he is a child
And I am still a girl
Not a woman yet
I don't think
I gave more than I was willing to lose
Here am I

Heavily invested
In a relationship that could be over
As quickly as it began
I love him more than he loves me
He could walk away and be fine
But me...
Well, I'm already a wreck
He is concerned with the happiness of the world
But what about me
What about himself
What about us
Doesn't matter I suppose
People pleasing isn't my thing
Don't want him to stay with me out of pity
Nor obligation
I want him to want me
To want to love me
For our love to be equal
Or for him to love me more...
If he loved me and I gave him nothing
Then I would have won
But I'm a loser
But this is a beautiful mistake
And loving him is my beautiful disaster

Perspective

I sat staring at her
Those beautiful light brown eyes
Still blurred with tears
That doused the flame that once
Burned only for me
Long multi-brown hair
Whipping her face
She is the best thing
That I've ever had in my life
And my mistake, my stupidity
Has driven her right over the edge
Of sanity and I can't
Grasp her hand fast enough...

I stood glaring at him
The befuddled look in his eyes
Like he had no clue that this would hurt
I love him so much
But I could just hurt him right now
Don't cry, don't let him see
I'm too good for him, I know
Still, I don't need to hear him say it
I can think of nothing but the time
He wasted, filled with empty promises
And I feel the urge,
Can't stop myself from
Striking his face repeatedly...

We lay silent
Tumbling over the past
The love that we once loved
What remains here now
Is the hope that trust isn't all lost
Falling over the words
Gathered between broken letters
And lovesick lullabies
We are nothing
Dressed up in the image
Of what we thought love was
But that wasn't it
Or was it?

There has to be more
We have to be more...
More than: our words
Our defenses
Our mistakes
Our stupidity
Our desires
Our behaviors
More than what we are portraying
A display of misplaced affection
Petty Boy-Girl scenario
That doesn't capture what love is
And only showcases what it is not

We are the nature of love
We just got lost on the way
Trying to become something more
Than romantic love
We are striving for agape
But ever falling short

INFATUATION

Getting High on You

I inject you
Feel you dominating my veins
Until the sting of you hits my cerebellum
Thoughts consumed of you in I
And parts of I in you
Offering pure pleasure
With the usual side effects
Swollen and soaked
I beg for another hit
Seeing you won't be enough
I've got to hear you speak
My heart leaps from rib cage
Into throat as you lean over
Arms outstretched
Gather what's left of my composed frame
Into pure salvation
The moment is too much
And I find myself
Overdosing on wishful thoughts
Your aroma and embrace
Pull away for instantaneous withdrawal
Mouth goes dry
Prohibiting speech
All that stumbles out of my mouth
Are meaningless expectancies
Give me that again
Please...
I am begging...
I'll quit after this
I swear

Getting High on You pt. 2

It feels good
If you've never been high
Then you can't understand
Whether it be natural
Or drug induced
He provokes my mind, my body
To that feeling
Something about inhaling his cologne
Feeling my body press into him
Having his arms encase me
It just feels **good**!!
I can't take it
He knows I can't take it
But he hugs me anyway
And the process takes place again
I've got to escape this
It's not wise for me to continue
But it feels so right
That I know it must be wrong

Unexpected

He had me speechless and trembling
I promised secrecy
But my body won't stop talking about it
Lips and mouth relay message to brain
Brain sends out jolts to the senses
Hands tremble
Body longs to release nervous energy
Eyes become moist
And I am trapped in the wreckage
Of everything that I can not reveal
Being un-nerved by his response
Un-mended and unprepared
I don't think that I was ready
But he sought to expose me
A child doing adult things
Jittery for hours to follow

50

Waiting to recuperate
From the sweet release
Of his physical assault
My intentions murdered
Then kissed back to life
My mouth a living memorial

Beautiful: A Working Definition

He is beautiful
Not by my traditional
Tall, chocolate, straight-from-the-field
Built like a sculpture of what a man should look like
Ideal of beautiful
But beautiful nonetheless
He's been described as an angelic beauty
Piercing blue eyes
I long for him to look into me
Wavy brown crown
Vanilla crème skin
I imagine the taste of his rosebud colored lips
Sweet like honey-marinated berries
Warm smile acting as a catalyst
Speeding the pace of my racing heart
Give him wings and I'm sure that he'll fly
No, ascend!
He could be my king
And I...
I am simply amazed
That he is so very beautiful
Not my normal football player
Too gorgeous to be gorgeous
So my natural type of beautiful
Still, effortlessly beautiful
Unlike any other being
Causes me to wonder if he's actual
I feel the heat radiating from his body
So he must be...
Radiant enough to spite the sun
A fine form, formed from nature

He would be the very definition of beautiful
If he were mine...
If he loved me...
If he met his own beauty

About a Boy

He is a god
Like a flawless diamond
Body of perfection
Beauty unmatched
He knows
But I am
Plain Jane
Brown-haired
Big-breasted
Brown-eyed
Brain
Fortunate to have him
Look and smile at me
I am young and naïve
He is mature and experienced
I want to serve him
Offer myself to him
If he'll have me
Swallow me down
But I am flawed...
Tainted by another
He deserves a virgin me
And I wouldn't deny him
Nor would I be denied
For only his lips can quench the thirst
Of my mouth
But he is far beyond my grasp
An angel
Sitting next to me
I am only human
When he is so much more
Sexuality personified
Sensuality innate
He is the answer

To my longing and desire
I want him
Like nothing else in the world
I need him
Like I need to breathe

Writing for Poetree

I wanted to write
A poem for you
But each time
I picked up the pencil
My hand would cramp up
My body would shake
The very thought of you
Makes still my heart
Writing for you is like
Trying to find my way in the dark
I need to touch the walls
The way I want to touch you
I need to smell my surroundings
The way I want to breathe you in
I need to taste the air
The way I want to taste your kiss
I need to listen to the sounds
The way I would listen
If you were talking to me
But you're not
So writing this has no point
And I have no hope
Forget about it
Put pencil away...
Stop attempting to...
Write for Poetree

Loving a Stranger

I'm in love with a stranger
I know him
But I don't *know* him
Does that take away from the fact
That I love him the way that people were meant to love?
Do I have to know his past
To understand that I want to love him forever?
Should the fact that we are strangers
Deny me the right to love him completely?
It shouldn't
I don't know all about him
But the first time that I saw him
I knew that I wanted to know him
When he first spoke to me
I knew that I wanted him
The first time I heard his poetry
I knew that I could love him
And if there was ever any doubt that I did love him
The first time that I kissed him assured me...
I am in love with this man...
A stranger...
I know that it's the truth
But does the stranger love me?
A question that strangers don't ask
Because they are strangers
The way that he and I are

The Love that I Love

It's sitting with you under the stars
Waiting for forever to come
But knowing that it's already here

Crying silent tears
Praying for the truth to shine through
Like His marvelous light

Being emotionally sick
Manifested into the physical nausea
Which refuses the wish of sleep

Pure madness
Unexplained and unwarranted
Dare to be reckless

A kiss/touch/look
That causes the world to freeze-frame
In the still photographs of memory

Laying beside you
Watching you sleep so peacefully
Living in your dreams

Knowing that home
Is only where you are
Or the last place that you left your heart

Putting myself on paper
To be exposed
And used however you want to

Saved by His mercy
Granted His Grace
Blessed by His favor

It's the love that I crave
That I need
I'd sacrifice for
I'd love enough to let go
See if it returns
In your eyes
In God's Kingdom
The love that I love is there

ABOUT THE AUTHOR

De'Borah Raquel

Trying to Write a De'Borah

this is indeed no easy task
full of little intricate twists and turns
so dramatic, trying to convey
a meaning that words can't say
everything is so delicately placed
positioned down to the dot
to state more appropriately down to
the last eye
yes that will do just fine
all this is accompanied by a look
sweet, innocent
no it must be a look of deep concentration
like one was trying to figure something out
one must also have an object on
which to be obsessed
with a perverted sickness
there would be no success
one has to stop and ponder with a
book deeply embedded under a chin
writing words that play and drip
                   off
                        of
                             the
                                   page

such a tender age and a menacing thing
trying to write a De'Borah
for it can't be done
at least not by me
i may have to kill her and drink her blood
to get that scary talent
maybe not

By Crystal L. Swain